Teens in

Australia

by Brenda Haugen

Content Adviser: Frances Cushing, MLS,
Research Associate, The Edward A. Clark Center
for Australian and New Zealand Studies,
The University of Texas at Austin

Reading Adviser: Katie Van Sluys, Ph.D.,
Department of Teacher Education,
DePaul University

Compass Point Books ◈ Minneapolis, Minnesota

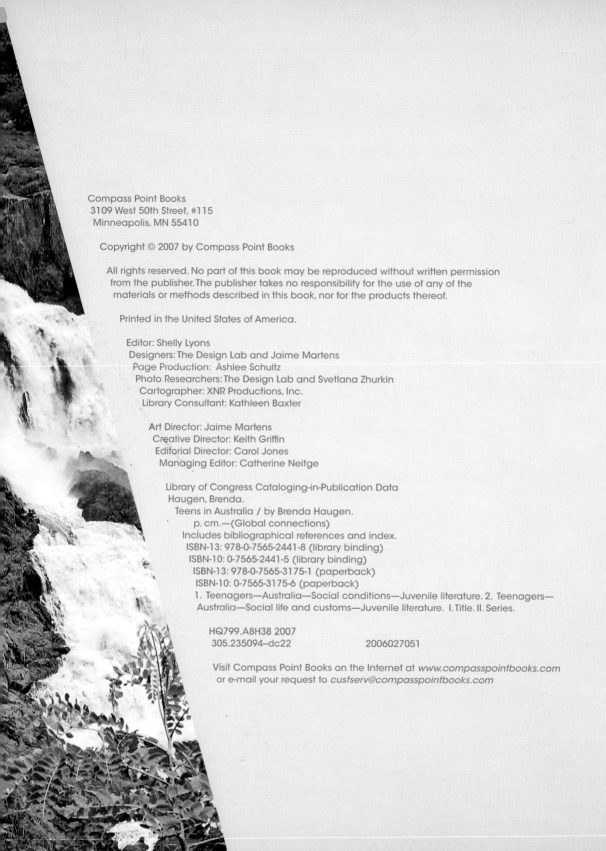

Compass Point Books
3109 West 50th Street, #115
Minneapolis, MN 55410

Printed in the United States of America.

Editor: Shelly Lyons
Designers: The Design Lab and Jaime Martens
Page Production: Ashlee Schultz
Photo Researchers: The Design Lab and Svetlana Zhurkin
Cartographer: XNR Productions, Inc.
Library Consultant: Kathleen Baxter

Art Director: Jaime Martens
Creative Director: Keith Griffin
Editorial Director: Carol Jones
Managing Editor: Catherine Neitge

Library of Congress Cataloging-in-Publication Data
Haugen, Brenda.
  Teens in Australia / by Brenda Haugen.
      p. cm.—(Global connections)
  Includes bibliographical references and index.
  ISBN-13: 978-0-7565-2441-8 (library binding)
  ISBN-10: 0-7565-2441-5 (library binding)
  ISBN-13: 978-0-7565-3175-1 (paperback)
  ISBN-10: 0-7565-3175-6 (paperback)
  1. Teenagers—Australia—Social conditions—Juvenile literature. 2. Teenagers—
  Australia—Social life and customs—Juvenile literature. I. Title. II. Series.

    HQ799.A8H38 2007
    305.235094—dc22   2006027051

Visit Compass Point Books on the Internet at www.compasspointbooks.com
or e-mail your request to custserv@compasspointbooks.com

Table of Contents

Huang

NORTH KOREA
SOUTH KOREA

Sea of
Japan

JAPAN

Yellow
Sea

East China
Sea

NEPAL

Ganges

INDIA

South
China
Sea

PHILIPPINES

PACIFIC

OCEAN

SRI LANKA

BRUNEI

MALAYSIA

INDONESIA

PAPUA NEW GUINEA

AUSTRALIA

INDIAN

OCEAN

Darling

Great
Australian
Bight

Tasman Sea

NEW ZEALAND

NEW CALEDONIA

FIJI

Canberra ⍟

LIFE FOR MOST AUSTRALIANS REVOLVES AROUND WATER. LOCATED BETWEEN THE SOUTH PACIFIC OCEAN AND THE INDIAN OCEAN, AUSTRALIA IS THE WORLD'S LARGEST ISLAND AND IS THE ONLY COUNTRY THAT IS ALSO A CONTINENT. The Australian government estimates that more than 20 million people live there, and approximately 1.8 million of them are teenagers. Nearly 85 percent of the total population lives in cities along the Australian coast and its beaches. Because they live so close to the ocean, teens often study the ocean in science classes, learn to protect it in some of their after-school clubs, and use it for recreation—swimming, sailing, and surfing with friends and family.

But for those living in the country's mainly desertlike interior, the lack of water rules their lives. Hundreds of miles may separate town from town, or even neighbor from neighbor. Water sources often dry up. Carrying an adequate supply of water can mean life or death to teens working or traveling in this area known as the Outback.

Australia boasts a 99 percent literacy rate, one of the best in the world.

1

School Days

LIKE MOST TEENAGERS, 14-YEAR-OLD BROOKE HILL RISES AROUND 7 A.M. ON WEEKDAYS. After dressing in her school uniform and grabbing a quick breakfast of cereal or yogurt, Hill heads for the bus stop and catches her ride to school.

Hill relies on public transportation to get to school, as do most teenagers in Australia. Getting a driver's license is a big deal for any teen, but Australians are usually at least 19 years old before earning a license.

Because the process takes so long, and because of the cost of maintaining a vehicle, most teens get around using public transportation, such as trams or buses. They also may catch rides with their parents or pedal their bikes to get from place to place.

Earning a License

Rules vary from state to state, but generally, at 16½, a teen can take a written test and apply for a learner license. With a learner license, a teen can drive only if accompanied by another person who has had a regular license for at least a year.

Beginners with a learner license can practice driving with their parents or other older licensed drivers. They also can take lessons through a professional learn-to-drive program. Learner licenses are good for a year.

When new drivers feel comfortable behind the wheel and understand the rules of the road, they can take the next step—a written and driving test. If the teen passes the test, he or she is given a provisional license, which is generally good for three years. The provisional license places limits on the driver. For instance, provisional drivers are bound by lower speed limits. After more experience behind the wheel—and taking another written and driving exam—a student finally can earn a full license with no restrictions.

Once at school, students gather in their homerooms. There teachers call the roll and read the day's announcements.

Children as young as 3 years old may go to preschool, but all Australians start elementary school the year of their sixth birthday. Primary, or elementary,

school begins with year one and runs through year six. High school, sometimes called college, spans years seven to 12.

Australia is divided into six states and two territories. The rules vary from state to state or territory, but most require students to stay in school through

Sweaters, polo shirts, and skirts or pants are common school uniforms throughout the country.

year 10, or age 15. About 10 percent of Australians quit school at the end of year 10. Some of those who leave go to a technical college or apprentice in a trade, while others will go straight into the work force.

As students get ready for school, most do not need to worry about what clothes to put on in the morning. Most schools, public and private, require students to wear uniforms. Each school has its own uniform.

"We have to wear uniforms, which are very long ankle-length dresses," said Rhiannon Hughes, a student at a private high school, St. Mary Star of the Sea College, in Wollongong, which is about 62 miles (99 kilometers) south of Sydney. "They are sometimes very annoying and hot in summer."

The dress code for schools in Melbourne can be especially strict. At one school, students must wear gray pants, a dark green wool sweater, and a white polo top. The sweater and polo each bear the school's crest. Shoes must be black leather with laces, and only a minimal amount of jewelry can be worn. There is some flexibility to the dress code, though. There are two types of dresses—summer and winter—that girls can wear. Also, shorts can be worn in the summer, and students have the choice between two types of winter jackets.

Of the 3 million students in Australia, about 1 million attend private schools. While public schools are free, almost all private schools charge tuition

In recent years, about 68 percent of students were attending public schools, about 20 percent were attending Roman Catholic schools, and about 12 percent were attending independent schools.

Religions in Australia

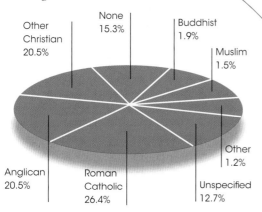

Other Christian 20.5%

None 15.3%

Buddhist 1.9%

Muslim 1.5%

Anglican 20.5%

Roman Catholic 26.4%

Unspecified 12.7%

Other 1.2%

Source: United States Central Intelligence Agency. *The World Factbook—Australia.*

and are run by religious institutions. However, students usually don't have to share the beliefs of the religion a school is associated with in order to attend.

For both public and private schools, the school day starts around 9 A.M. and runs until about 3 P.M. Most schools give students two recess breaks—one in the morning and one in the afternoon—that usually are 15 to 30 minutes long.

Lunchtime is generally around noon or 1 P.M.,

and lasts from 45 minutes to an hour. Schools usually have a canteen, or cafeteria, that sells hot foods, salads, beverages, meat pies, and sweets. Students usually eat on the school grounds, but some schools allow year 12 students to leave the school for lunch. They may go to a cafe or the local shopping center to grab something to eat. If students have time after lunch before their next class, they might visit the school's library, rehearse music, play basketball or other sports, or just sit and talk with friends.

In high school, students typically have six classes per day. Among Brooke Hill's classes are science, geography, history, English, math, a computer course, and physical education (P.E.). Because she goes to a Catholic school, she is required to take a religion class. The best part of school, though, according to Hill's classmate Michelle Glossop, is something called sport. "Our school has P.E. three times a week, but every second Friday, from 1:30 to 3:15, we have sport," she said. "This is by far the best day of the week."

Physical education classes sometimes include rugby, one of the most popular sports in Australia.

In her class, the students are given a list of activities to choose from, including surfing, yoga, martial arts, volleyball, tennis, basketball, and golf.

School Terms

The school year varies from state to state, but generally begins in January or February and ends in December. Most states divide the school year into four terms, with short vacations usually in April, late June, and late September. The December break is centered on summer in Australia.

"Our school year consists of four terms of about eight to 11 weeks, and at the end of each term we have two weeks of holidays," said Rhiannon Hughes, a private school student. "At the end of the fourth term, we have six weeks for Christmas holidays … in December and January."

Large high schools in cities such as Sydney may serve as many as 1,400 students. The smallest may have just 200 students. Typical high schools, however, have an enrollment of 500 to 800 students.

Some schools offer tennis as a physical education class, but clubs also offer classes for teens.

Australian Seasons

Australians use the same 12-month calendar as countries in the Northern Hemisphere. They also celebrate holidays such as Christmas and Easter, but the seasons could not be more different than those ocurring in the Northern Hemisphere.

Earth is divided in two halves by the equator. The top half is called the Northern Hemisphere, while everything below the equator is the Southern Hemisphere. Orbiting the sun, Earth is inclined at an angle of 23.5 degrees. When it is summer in the Northern Hemisphere, northern latitudes receive more sunlight, making the days longer and the angle of the sun higher. Meanwhile, days are shorter and the weather is cooler in the Southern Hemisphere. Countries that are close to the equator experience little change and remain hot throughout the year. Eventually, as Earth continues its orbit, the sun will shine more on the opposite side of the planet, reversing the seasons.

Because Australia is in the Southern Hemisphere, seasonal holidays such as Christmas and New Year's fall during Australia's warm period. Australian students are given a summer vacation to be with their families, and many families celebrate by going to the beach.

Australian Seasons

Summer:	December through February
Autumn:	March through May
Winter:	June through August
Spring:	September through November

Source: Australian Government Culture and Recreation Portal. *Australian Weather and the Seasons.*

Students gather on a playground at South Sydney School.

The size of each class also varies. Required classes are usually large, but other optional classes, known as electives, have a smaller class size. However, only older students have these choices. In years seven and eight, all students take the same courses, such as math, science, and English. Beginning in year nine, students can choose some of their courses. By the time they are in years 11 and 12, students at Gladstone Park, for example, are only required to take English. They choose all their other courses from those offered by their school. They base their choices on what they plan to do in the future. For example, if a student wants to become a doctor, he or she may choose to take more science courses. Universities also may require certain courses, such as foreign languages, if students want to be considered for admittance.

More choices may be a reward for growing older, but students in the upper grades also take on more responsibility. Students are tested in every year of school. But the tests taken by older students are more difficult and more important.

In public schools, students usually have special exams beginning in year 10. These exams test whether the students are learning what the school expects them to learn. The grades from the exams are added to the results from the work the students have done throughout the rest of the year.

After year 10, students may choose to take vocational education classes. These classes offer training in a wide range of occupations and are usually cheaper than university courses. Vocational, or career specific, training is provided through government-run institutions called Technical and Further Education schools, or TAFEs. Students may go on to a university after two years with credits from a TAFE that meets a university's requirements.

At the end of year 12, students take a final exam called the Higher School Certificate (HSC). The HSC is worth half of a student's final year grade. The other half of the grade is based on the coursework the student did during the year. All students in a state or territory

A teen in New South Wales studies at her kitchen table.

take the same test. The scores students receive go toward their entrance score if they plan to go on to a university. About 29 percent of Australians continue their educations after high school. Entrance into the country's universities is very competitive, so students want to earn the highest HSC scores they can.

Today many high school students look forward to focusing on the newer areas of communication, marketing, and advertising, though interest continues to grow in careers in medicine, law, economics, and the environment.

The end of year 12 is a time for celebration for students, parents, and teachers. Throughout Australia, a high school graduate is called a *schoolie*. In New South Wales, after the HSC has been taken, there is a schoolies week, during which students are allowed to leave school to go to parties, to the beach, or sometimes even on cruises.

To mark the end of high school, many schools will have formal dinners for the students. A three-course meal, a DJ, and

schoolie
SKOOL-ee

In recent years, about 82 percent of 15- to 21-year-olds were attending an educational institution full time.

Australian Universities

There are 39 government-funded universities and two private universities in Australia. Tuition can be paid in advance at a small discount, or a student can get a loan from the Australian government. Although the government pays the loan directly to the university, the student must pay this money back. When the student graduates from a university and reaches a certain income level, the loan payments are taken out of his or her salary.

Founded in 1850, the University of Sydney was Australia's first university.

prizes enhance an evening where staff members wish the students a bright and prosperous future.

High schools also host graduation ceremonies. These are formal affairs where parents gather to celebrate their children's accomplishments. A valedictorian, chosen by the school's administrators, gives a speech. A guest speaker, usually a successful graduate of years past, also talks to the graduates and their parents. Many schools serve food and beverages before and after the event, but the biggest parties are hosted by the students and their parents. After-graduation parties are popular throughout Australia. Sometimes graduates host them at their homes or go to nightclubs.

Dancing the Night Away

Most schools host dances—sometimes called discos or socials—for students. Many schools will have a social for students in year 10. Although it is supervised by the teachers, the social is

Students gather on the beach at Mornington Port Phillip Bay in Victoria.

organized by the student body. During a three-course meal, a disc jockey plays music, and the students dance between courses. Girls put a lot of effort into choosing a dress, having their hair done, and putting on makeup. Even the boys will work on their appearance for the social. The event is limited to the students who go to the school.

In year 11, many schools organize a debutante ball, which is similar to a prom. Students usually plan to attend the event with another person, and couples will practice dancing for many weeks before the event. Students dress formally, with the girls in dresses and the boys in black suits. To tie in with the formal evening, it is popular for a couple to arrive in a limo. Families will reserve a table at the ball and even take part in the dancing by the end of the evening. The dance will usually end around midnight, but a few unofficial parties usually follow.

Teens prepare for a graduation formal.

Schools that are restricted to just boys or just girls still have dances. They just pair up with other schools. For instance, St. Mary Star of the Sea College, an all-girls high school, pairs up for dances with a nearby all-boys school called Edmund Rice.

"For year nine, it happens once a term," student Michelle Glossop said. "There is a theme. At our last disco, it was 'Occupations.' It went from 7 to 10 P.M. There was a DJ, and everyone had a really great night. It was fun seeing everyone all dressed up [as if they worked in different occupations]. In year nine, it's just a casual dance where we get a chance to meet new people, but in year 10, there is something called a formal where we bring a date, get all dressed up, and some people even arrive in a limo. Year 12 also has a formal as part of them celebrating leaving school."

After-School Activities

Australian students may join a variety of after-school activities, and sometimes they are offered at no cost to the student. For instance, the Australian Sports Commission recently started the Active After-School Communities Program (AASC) as part of the government's drive to reduce childhood obesity. The AASC offers structured physical activities for primary school students. Some schools offer music, drama programs, and sports teams, but often these activities are sponsored

Boys play Australian rules football in western Australia.

by community organizations or clubs rather than by schools.

"Outside of school, I play soccer on Sunday mornings, and we train two times during the week," said Rhiannon Hughes. "I am in the under-15 girls team and play for our local Thirroul junior soccer club. Soccer is very popular with girls, and we play soccer during autumn and winter from April through August." Girls often play field hockey as well.

According to Jane Myers, the public liaison for one of Sydney's high schools, most boys play Australian rules football outside of school on the weekends. Although there are interschool competitions during the school day, the only people who watch are the students. Private schools, however, traditionally hold competitions with other private schools on Saturday mornings. These events usually draw a large number of spectators.

Some school activities revolve around improving communities and the environment. For example, Michelle Glossop is part of her school's Conservation Club, a group of students who are active in keeping the environment clean. She's also a member of a club called Duke of Edinburgh. This group requires members to participate

The Duke of Edinburgh Program

Young people ages 14 through 25 can win awards through the Duke of Edinburgh program. They can earn bronze, silver, or gold awards by meeting several requirements. They include providing useful service to others, developing personal interests and practical skills, participating in physical recreation and improving physical skills and health, and following a spirit of adventure and discovery. To earn the gold award, the top level of the program, participants must take on a residential project with the goal of broadening their experience by working with others in a community setting.

The Waterwatch Programme in Victoria uses volunteers from the community to teach students how to monitor pollution in the area's bodies of water.

in community service as well as fun physical fitness activities, such as hiking.

Learning in the Outback

Away from the coastal cities and towns lies the Outback. Though it covers nearly 80 percent of Australia, it includes only about 10 percent of the nation's population.

The Outback consists of deserts and grasslands. Large areas are used as stations—ranches where sheep or cattle are raised. Australia leads the world in raising sheep and producing wool. Sheep outnumber people in Australia by about 10 to one.

A worker at a station in New South Wales counts sheep.

Because the Outback boasts little vegetation, stations need to be huge in order to support the livestock. It is not unusual for a station to include more than half a million acres (200,000 hectares). Some stations are the size of whole countries in Europe.

Stations in the Outback can be very isolated. Hundreds of miles may separate a station from its nearest neighbor.

Because classmates live so far apart, educating students in the Outback presents a special challenge. To solve the problem, Australians came up with Schools of the Air, which are now called Schools of Distance Education (SDE).

Through SDE, students living in the Outback receive lessons and

First School of the Air

The first School of the Air was in Alice Springs. It officially opened June 8, 1951. At first, lessons were broadcast over the radio just one way—teachers talked while the students listened. Three half-hour lessons were broadcast each week. In time, two-way communication allowed students to ask and answer questions, too.

While the schools continue to use radio as a tool, they also use phones, e-mail, Internet, fax machines, video, and mail.

Today there are 12 Schools of Distance Education. They serve a total of about 1,000 students. The Alice Springs School of the Air includes a staff of 14 teachers, who are responsible for educating about 140 students spread across about 400,000 square miles (1 million sq km) in central Australia.

Australia
Topographical
Map

send homework through the mail or through e-mail. They communicate with their teachers using two-way radios, telephones, e-mail, and instant messaging. Each student is required to have a tutor. Usually a parent will fill the role.

Charleville, an SDE school in Queensland, serves students from preschool to year 10. Those who wish to continue their education beyond year 10 can take courses with the Brisbane School of Distance Education, another SDE, or go to boarding school.

The year-seven students served by Charleville Distance Education

Teen Scenes

Fifteen-year-old Michelle Glossop runs from one activity to the next. Because her mother works just across the street from the school, she drives Michelle and her twin sister, Ali, to St. Mary Star of the Sea College in Wollongong, where the teens are in year 9. After a busy day of learning about mathematics, history, English, geography, and science, Michelle usually has a club or sports activity after school. But today is Saturday, and Michelle and her tennis team are competing against others from all across Wollongong. Afterward, Michelle meets Ali, who is learning to play basketball, and they shoot hoops for about an hour. Later on, they might meet up with some of their other friends and go to the beach or to the shopping mall. Because most of her friends live within biking distance from her house, Michelle might just ride to a friend's house, where they will watch movies and eat pizza.

Seventh-grader Emily Flder lives on a cattle station in a remote area of Queensland. She rises early in the morning to have breakfast before heading outside to help with chores. By 7:30 A.M., she is cleaning out stables and feeding horses. She has no time to waste. At 8:45 A.M., school starts. She gathers her homework and sits down with her mother to begin the day's lessons. At around 10 A.M., Emily takes a short break for tea before resuming her schoolwork. At 1 P.M., she has lunch, followed by about 45 minutes of reading. The rest of her afternoon is spent riding horses or helping her father make sure the cattle have enough food. Because the area has not had a significant rainy season for many years, the land is very dry, leaving little natural vegetation for the cattle to eat. When the chores are done, Emily helps feed, wash, and groom the horses before having a chance to run around the yard and play with her two sisters. After eating their evening meal around 8 P.M., the girls brush their teeth and head to bed to get a good night's sleep.

A teen in the Aboriginal settlement of Toomelah, New South Wales, lives in a small old home with 10 other members of his family. Only 35 houses dot the landscape of the community of 350 people. Twenty years ago, 500 people lived in Toomelah, but the settlement is slowly dying. Elders in the community want to teach young people about their heritage, but few seem to listen anymore. Teens are more concerned about survival. Jobs are difficult to find, and few teens in Toomelah finish high school.

Students work in a remote schoolroom in South Australia.

study many subjects, including art, English, grammar, Japanese, and math. They also have health and physical education. At least once a year they gather to spend time with their teachers and classmates. Called minischools, these gatherings are hosted by families in the SDE program and usually last three days. Teachers, students, and tutors all travel to the host family's station and sleep in bunkhouses or tents. The minischools give the students a chance to talk and play with students their own age—something that might

rarely happen otherwise. Teachers often plan special activities that include guest speakers. It's an opportunity for teachers to expose their students to a world they might not otherwise experience. A guest speaker might be an author or illustrator of children's books, an African dancer, or a sports coach.

Surveys show that teenagers living outside the capital cities of Australia's states, particularly in the more remote Outback areas, are less likely to go on to a university. They may find full-time employment where they are living.

The average family in Australia has one or two children, but some are larger.

2

Typical Teen Life

TYPICAL AUSTRALIAN FAMILY STRUCTURES INCLUDE TWO-PARENT HOUSEHOLDS, single-parent families, and stepfamilies. Sometimes grandparents live with their families, too.

About two-thirds of families own their homes. A common dwelling is a one-story house made of brick with a tile roof. A two-story house was once considered by many to be a luxury. Today more people own larger homes. Most homes have their own yards and gardens. About one in 10 homes has a pool.

In the hotter northern part of Australia, many houses are built on stumps, or stilts. The stumps allow air to flow under the house to keep the inside cooler. The stumps also protect

Common housing in Sydney includes town houses that are built close together.

the homes from flooding, particularly during the summer and autumn months, when cyclones or monsoons can drop as much as 40 inches (1,016 millimeters) of rain in a single day.

Teens help take care of their houses and families. Many teens have chores to do each day. A teen may take care of the family pet and clean his or her bedroom. Some teens help cook dinner and hang out clothes to dry on a clothesline. Teens may get weekly allowances for helping around the house. In the Sydney and Melbourne suburbs, teens may get an allowance of 25 to 50 Australian dollars (U.S.$20 to $39). Teenagers use their allowance for transportation to school—buses or inner-city trains—or for lunches and snacks. They might lose that allowance, be grounded, or have television or computer privileges taken away if they break their parents' rules or do not do their chores.

In their day-to-day lives, Australians use a unique language they call Strine, a word that was created from a pronunciation of the word *Australian*. Strine is a version of English, but Australians often shorten words to create new ones. They also tend to add an "ee" or "o" sound to the end of shortened words. For

example, they call a politician a *polly*, and the word *breakfast* is turned into *brekkie*.

Food

Australian tucker, or food, is a unique blend of traditions. The diverse population prepares many kinds of food. As a result, Australian tucker is a combination of

polly
PAH-lee

brekkie
BRECK-ee

Australian Currency

Australia's unit of money is the Australian dollar. The country's money includes coins and bills. Australia was the first nation to use plastic to make its money. Australian bills are printed on

thin plastic instead of paper. The bills last four times as long as paper money, and they provide greater security against counterfeiting.

many flavors and cooking styles.

A typical breakfast consists of bacon and eggs, cereal and orange juice, or something more Australian, like Vegemite, a dark brown salty spread made from brewers' yeast extract.

"I usually eat Vegemite on toast or Nutella on toast with a glass of juice," Rhiannon Hughes said. Nutella is a hazelnut and chocolate spread that originated in Italy.

Lunchtime meals are usually light. Salads, sandwiches, and meat pies are common fare. Afternoon snacks of lamingtons—small, square cakes dipped in chocolate and rolled in coconut—or little pancakes called *pikelets* with cups of tea tide most people over until their evening meals.

Many families eat their evening meals together. They may gather around the dining room table and eat while talking about the day's events. A typical meal includes meat, potatoes, and a vegetable. Asian, Greek, and Italian dishes and spices are popular. Eggplant, zucchini, shiitake mushrooms, garlic, and bok choy were brought to Australia by immigrants but are now

pickelets
PICK-eh-lets

Vegemite, an excellent source of Vitamin B, is eaten as a spread on toast and sandwiches.

commonly found in Australian dishes. Especially on the weekends, families may gather outside and enjoy a meal fresh from the *barbie,* or barbecue. Favorite grilled foods include fish, shellfish, chicken, and lamb chops. Dessert often includes fresh fruit, such as apples, bananas, oranges, papayas or pineapple. Another popular treat is *pavlova,* a concoction of meringue, cream, and fruit.

barbie
BAHR-bee

pavlova
pahv-LOH-vah

Health Care

Australians love to eat, and many enjoy sweets. However, many citizens also take care of their health, visiting doctors and dentists regularly.

All Australian citizens can get health care through a program called Medicare, which is paid for using taxes on people's incomes. Medicare covers most doctors' fees and care in public hospitals.

While most teens see themselves

At the beach, teens make meals on the barbie.

Although the percentage of teens who smoke has recently dropped, the habit is still a problem among the teenage population.

as being in good health, they face health problems as well. Among the widespread problems is excessive alcohol consumption. Four out of five high school students report using alcohol, which can lead to other problems, such as alcoholism and accidents resulting from drunken driving.

Another health concern for Australian teens is drug abuse. Marijuana is the most commonly used illegal drug by teenagers. More than one-third of teens report using marijuana at least once. Between 4 percent and 9 percent of teens report using other drugs, including amphetamines, cocaine, ecstasy, and hallucinogens. Male teens are more likely than females to try illegal drugs.

Cigarettes remain popular among Australian teenagers as well, but their use is declining, thanks in part to massive media campaigns. In 1984, 17 percent of 12- to 14-year-olds reported smoking cigarettes. By 2002, that number had dropped to 9 percent. Teenagers who smoke and drink are more likely to experiment with illegal drugs than are those who don't use cigarettes or alcohol.

The Royal Flying Doctor Service

Australia's cities boast modern hospitals and high-quality health care. However, for those living in the Outback, clinics and hospitals may be hundreds of miles away. In 1928, Australians came up with a unique solution—the Royal Flying Doctor Service (RFDS). The RFDS provides 24-hour emergency care to people living in the Outback. More than 500 people work for the RFDS, which has 22 bases in Australia's interior. About 40 aircraft are always ready to fly health-care workers wherever they are needed. Each day, an average of 71 patients are taken from the Outback to hospitals equipped to care for them. In addition, the RFDS supplies more than 3,500 medical chests. These chests are stocked with a variety of important drugs and medical supplies that might be needed to save a life. The chests are scattered in the sparsely populated areas of Australia, including isolated stations, remote mining sites, and lighthouses. The RFDS also has regular clinics that offer immunizations, dental care, eye exams, and routine health exams. RFDS doctors and nurses are also available by radio and telephone to answer health questions. In an average year, the RFDS helps about 200,000 patients through its many services.

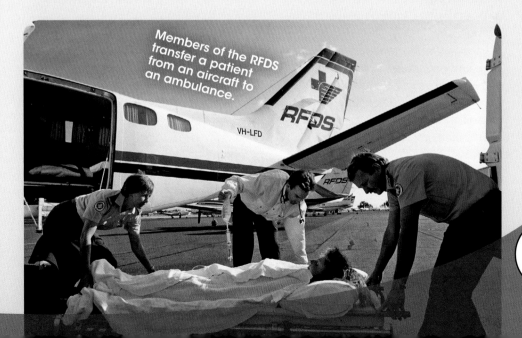

Members of the RFDS transfer a patient from an aircraft to an ambulance.

39

Most public areas are supposed to be smoke free, but there are some licensed indoor areas that still allow smoking.

NO SMOKING
Smoke-free Environment Act 2000

Teens also may struggle with body image. Childhood and teenage obesity in Australia has tripled in the last 10 years. Teenagers who dislike their bodies may resort to dangerous diets and develop eating disorders.

Suicide is the second most common cause of death among Australian teens. Only car accidents claim more teen lives. While young women are more likely to try suicide, young men are more likely to succeed in taking their own lives. Since the mid-1970s, the suicide rate for males ages 15 to 24 has tripled. The suicide rate for young men living in rural areas is twice that of those living in cities.

Australian teens do have people to turn to for help and support. All state schools and most private schools have counselors available to their students. Teens may go to counselors to discuss any of their problems—from smoking and drug use to eating disorders and problems at home. The counselors can offer resources to help teens with their addictions or other problems.

Fighting Against Obesity

Obesity rates in Australia have doubled in the last 20 years. In 2006, one in four high school students in Australia was overweight or obese. It is projected that by 2020 75 percent of Australia's population will be overweight or obese.

About three billion Australian dollars (U.S.$2.4 billion) a year goes into the direct cost of treating overweight or obese people in Australia. Obesity can lead to an increased chance of heart disease, cancer, diabetes, asthma, dementia, hypertension, and arthritis.

In 2004, the Australian government had spent more than 147 million Australian dollars (U.S.$116 million) over four years just on programs aimed at families and schools to promote nutrition and physical activities.

Aborigines make up about 2.4 percent of Australia's total population.

3

A Mix of Cultures

THE FIRST PEOPLE CAME TO AUSTRALIA ABOUT 40,000 YEARS AGO. Scientists believe these native people, called Aborigines, traveled to Australia by boat from Southeast Asia, the closest land mass inhabited by people at that time.

Most Aborigines lived in the coastal areas and were seminomadic, moving to where there were food sources at certain times of the year. Aborigines in the Outback were nomadic, relying on their knowledge of water sources to survive.

In 1770, before Britain's Captain James Cook charted the east coast of Australia, it has been estimated that there were between 300,000 and 500,000 Aborigines. During early colonial times, disease, the taking of Aboriginal lands and water resources, and a wave of massacres in the 1800s reduced their population to about 60,000 by 1900.

Today's Aboriginal population is around 458,520. About 127,000 Aboriginal children attend primary and secondary schools in Australia. The great majority of Aborigines live in suburban areas on the east coast, but there also are Aboriginal settlements in the Outback.

Today most Australians are relatively new to the country. About 40 percent of Australians are either immigrants or children of immigrants. Since 1945, more than 5 million people from nearly 200 countries have moved to the island nation. They have brought with them their traditions, favorite foods, and other

A group of Aboriginal teens live in the Kununurra area of Western Australia.

Arnhem Land Aboriginal Reserve

Aborigines make up approximately 25 percent of the Northern Territory population. They live on 15 Aboriginal reserves. The largest is Arnhem Land. The reserve has an area of 37,000 square miles (96,200 sq km) and is located in the northernmost portion of the territory. Its northern coast consists of mangrove swamps and tidal rivers flowing from the ocean. The rest of the reserve is covered with tropical jungles, swamps, and gorges. The area draws many tourists since it is connected to Kakadu National Park, the second largest national park in the world. Only Northeast Greenland National Park is larger. More than 230,000 tourists visit Kakadu each year. Along with its beautiful landscape and a wide variety of wildlife, Kakadu is home to a large collection of Aboriginal rock art and artifacts.

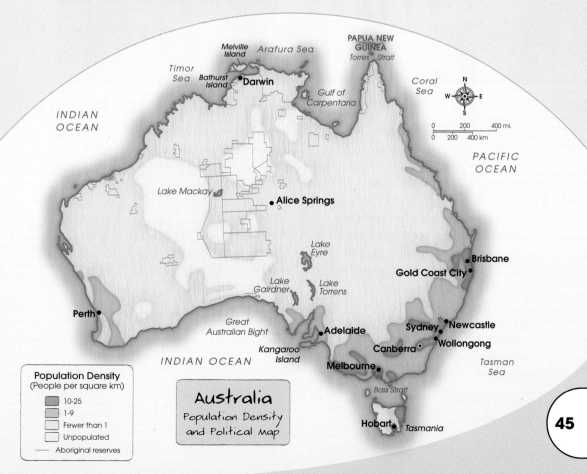

Australia
Population Density and Political Map

Population Density
(People per square km)

- 10-25
- 1-9
- Fewer than 1
- Unpopulated
- — Aboriginal reserves

Aborigines hold up the unofficial Aboriginal flag during a land rights protest in Sydney.

LAND IS LIFE

parts of their culture, which have now become a part of Australia's culture.

"We need to share our country with others, but also unashamedly want the talent, energy and industry of diverse groups of immigrants, to help us develop a potential which is plainly abundant," said Jerzy Zubzycki, a Polish-born former professor at the Australian National University.

In the past, some Australians of European descent failed to live peacefully with the Aborigines. But understanding of the Aboriginal culture has grown. In recent decades, efforts have been made to make up for wrongs committed against the Aborigines in the past, including giving back some of their sacred lands.

Family

Australian teens are often very close to their families, and younger teens in particular, spend a great deal of time with their parents.

Saturdays are usually devoted to sports or recreation. Parents often serve as coaches or referees for their teens' games, whether they be soccer, field hockey, football, cricket, or another sport. If parents are not participating as coaches or referees, they are often found on the sidelines, cheering for their children and their teams.

Sunday reigns as a day for family and friends. Church does not play a big role for most Australians. Teens and their families are more likely to be found at the beach or having a picnic or barbecue with their extended families

Teens might spend time with their parents at the beach.

and friends at a park or in a back yard.

Although teens enjoy spending time with their parents, they also enjoy going places on their own. Since most cities have buses and other public transportation, teens can go to the beach, the museum, or the mall without having to rely on their parents to get them there.

Twins Michelle and Ali Glossop keep in touch with their friends outside of school by talking on their cell phones or chatting online. About 45 percent of 13- to 15-year-olds in Australia have mobile phones.

"Almost everyone has a cell phone to keep in contact with friends when you're out, or to ring their parents when you're out, so they know where you are," Michelle Glossop said.

Australian teens love spending time with friends. They have sleepovers, go shopping, go to movies, or hang out at the beach.

Teens surf the waves in Rainbow Bay near Brisbane.

Days at the Beach

Since most Australian teens live near the ocean, one of their favorite destinations is the beach.

"We usually spend the whole or half a day there," said Rhiannon Hughes. "Along the beach there are places to eat, like kiosks and cafes. They mostly sell fish and chips [french fries], hamburgers, and ice cream. At the beach we mostly swim in the ocean and the rock pools. Last [school break], I went to a surfing school with my friends. We went out into the surf for about two or three hours and got taught how to surf by instructors."

On Australia's hot summer days, the beaches are crowded, especially on weekends. The fine white sand is dotted with youths lying on the sand or on colorful beach towels. Teens dress in swimsuits in nearly every color and style.

Most of the popular beaches are marked with flags that show where it is safe to swim. Lifeguards also stand watch at many beaches.

Along with surfing on boards, teens

can also be seen body surfing and riding the waves on boogie boards. However, they are more likely to be lying on the beach with their friends and talking, soaking up the sun, walking along the beach searching for shells, or listening to music.

Bondi Beach near Sydney and Surfer's Paradise near Brisbane rank among Australia's most popular beaches. Along with swimming and surfing, teens here can enjoy sailing and fishing, too. Some teens also like snorkeling. Armed with a mask,

breathing tube, and flippers, young people can explore an underwater world of stunning coral and multicolored fish without having to come up for air as they do when they are swimming.

Surfer's Paradise is part of Australia's Gold Coast, a stretch of beautiful seashore that runs along the coast of Queensland just south of Brisbane. With warm temperatures and sunshine about 245 days a year, the Gold Coast welcomes beach lovers almost year-round.

Teens celebrate a birthday by lighting sparklers at a beach in Sydney.

4

Holidays Down Under

AUSTRALIANS LOVE A GOOD CELEBRATION AND CELEBRATE SEVERAL HOLIDAYS DURING THE YEAR. Some are religious holidays, and others are unique to Australia. Some are national holidays, and some are celebrated only in certain states or communities. Christmas, sometimes called *Chrissie*, is the day

Christians celebrate the birth of Jesus Christ. It is also celebrated as a national holiday in Australia. Christmas is in the summer for Australians. As a result, Christmas celebrations are often held outdoors. On December 25, the beaches of

Chrissie
KRIS-see

People gather at Cairns Central Shopping Mall in northern Queensland to do their Christmas shopping.

Sydney are dotted with families soaking in the summer sun. Dressed in swimming suits of every imaginable color, parents and children lie on their towels and laugh, chat, and relax together. A teen listens to the new iPod she unwrapped that morning and already has loaded with songs by her favorite bands, such as Green Day, Switchfoot, Silverchair, and Good Charlotte. Her toes wiggle to the beat. Her little brother points toward the ocean with a gasp of surprise. Is that Santa surfing? Indeed it is—someone wearing the famous red and white outfit is riding the waves.

Homes may be decorated for the

holiday with ferns and Christmas bells, which are flowers that blossom in reddish-orange blooms.

"At Christmas, all of my family comes down, and we have a party," said Rhiannon Hughes. "We chop down a Christmas tree … and decorate it."

Family members rise in the morning and exchange gifts at breakfast. After church, they have a delicious, traditional Christmas meal, complete with a roast turkey or lamb and all the fixings, including potatoes and gravy and cranberry sauce. Then they usually head to the beach or a park and enjoy the rest of the day together.

Other National Holidays

Along with Christmas, Easter is also a national holiday. Christians in Australia

Christmas celebrations can be seen throughout the country, even at Bondi Beach in Sydney.

National Holidays

Public holidays in Australia vary from region to region, but some are celebrated nearly everywhere.

New Year's Day—**January 1**	
Australia Day—**January 26**	
Good Friday, Easter, and Easter Monday— **March or April**	
ANZAC Day— **April 25**	
Queen's Birthday—**Second Monday in June**	
Christmas—**December 25**	
Boxing Day—**December 26**	

pointed nose, and a long tail like a rat's tail, with a white tip. They are unique to Australia, living primarily in the northern areas of the country.

Many people like to go to the Royal Easter Show in Sydney. Once simply a display of farm produce, it has grown to become

and around the world consider Easter the holiest day of the year. It marks the day they believe Jesus Christ rose from the dead.

Easter falls on a Sunday in March or April, depending on the Christian calendar. The Friday before Easter— known as Good Friday—and Easter Monday—the day following the Easter celebration—are both national holidays as well.

Some families celebrate Easter by going to church. Many families enjoy a noontime feast, usually of lamb. Children hunt for Easter eggs and candy. In Easter baskets, Australian children get Easter *bilbies* instead of Easter bunnies. Bilbies have long ears, a

bilbies
BILL-bees

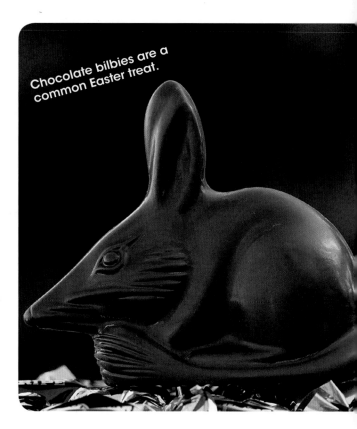

Chocolate bilbies are a common Easter treat.

A crowd watches the Grande Parade, in which more than 700 animals and their owners march, at Sydney's Royal Easter Show.

a national show of all things Australian. There are also competitions, such as the Sydney Royal Rodeo.

Australia Day falls on January 26. It marks the day in 1788 when Captain Arthur Phillip arrived in Sydney Cove with the First Fleet from Britain. Although Captain Cook had explored the eastern coastline of Australia in the early 1770s, no colonies were established then. The First Fleet carried 1,000 passengers, many of whom were convicts. Their crimes often included nothing worse than stealing a loaf of bread. By 1853, convicts were no longer being sent to Australia, and the

Invasion Day

Although Australia Day is a national holiday, not everyone agrees on its meaning. For example, the Aborigines see it as "Invasion Day," because of how their ancestors were treated by the new settlers. In 1788, the first European colony in New South Wales was established. Aborigines were exposed to new diseases, which depleted their numbers. They also had their lands taken from them and were forced to integrate into white society. Much of the Aboriginal culture was lost. Recently some indigenous Australians have celebrated January 26 as "Survival Day," thankful that their ancestors were not completely wiped out by colonization.

Others think Australia Day should be held on January 1, because on that day in 1901, the six colonies joined to become the six states of the Commonwealth of Australia. Though it remained part of the British Commonwealth, the new nation created its own central government, led by a prime minister.

A re-enactment of the British landing in Sydney Harbour takes place on Australia Day.

continent had been divided into six separate colonies.

Australia Day is celebrated with parades, picnics, and fireworks. In Sydney, the British landing is re-enacted in Sydney Harbour, and cannons are fired.

On April 25, Australians celebrate ANZAC Day. The holiday is named for

the Australian and New Zealand Army Corps (ANZAC) that fought in World War I, but it honors all the country's veterans.

On ANZAC Day, soldiers and veterans of all ages lead parades to war memorials. Nearly every town has a memorial to its veterans. Brass bands play in the parades. Many veterans wear the traditional slouch hats associated with Australian soldiers. They wear the hats with the left sides of the brims cocked up to allow rifles to rest on their shoulders. Children often march beside their fathers and grandfathers. ANZAC Day is an emotional day filled with speeches remembering those lost to war.

Veterans often march in parades to honor ANZAC Day.

The queen of England, Queen Elizabeth II, remains the queen of Australia. Since Australia became a federation in 1901, she is no longer directly involved in the Australian government. But she is a part of everyday life there—her image appears on the Australian five-dollar bill. On the second Monday in June, Australians celebrate the Queen's Birthday.

The queen's birthday is actually April 21, but it is traditional for monarchs to have official birthdays different from their actual birthdays. By celebrating the queen's official birthday in June, Australians get a holiday break before the start of winter.

The final national holiday of the year lands on the day after Christmas. December 26 is known as Boxing Day.

This holiday gives Australians an extra day to relax and enjoy more time with friends and family. It is a tradition that traces back to England. Boxing Day was first celebrated in England as a special day set aside for the wealthy to give small boxes of money, clothing, or other gifts to their servants as bonuses for all the work they did for the family during the year.

Celebrations

Birthdays are cause for celebration in Australia. Birthdays are a family affair, complete with cake, balloons, and gifts for young children. As children grow older, they may invite friends to their birthday parties. Older teens may still celebrate with their families but also enjoy time at the beach or movies to celebrate their special day with friends. They also might host birthday barbecues, pizza parties, dance parties, or sleepovers. Birthday gifts for teens include a variety of items but some sought-after gifts are electronic gadgets, such as MP3 players and cell phones.

Weddings are another special time to be spent with family and friends. Weddings range from formal affairs at churches to more casual events at the beach, a park, or a garden. People must be at least 16 years old to get married. Most couples have a maid of honor and a best man to serve as witnesses and sign the marriage documents.

It is common for people to hold receptions after their weddings. At the

Patriotic Duty

Australians take their patriotic duties very seriously. Among those duties is voting. All citizens are eligible to vote when they turn 18. In fact, voting is required. If a person fails to vote, the Australian Electoral Commission sends a letter asking the person to either provide a valid reason for not voting or pay a $20 fine. If the person ignores the letter, the fine grows and can result in a court appearance.

Many couples choose to have a wedding photograph taken near the Sydney Opera House.

reception, guests can congratulate the newly married couple and share a meal and wedding cake with them. The cake may be the traditional white tiered cake, a chocolate cake, or even an ice cream cake or cheesecake. The reception is usually followed by a dance.

Family and friends also gather for sad occasions, such as funerals. A funeral can be as unique as the person whose life it celebrates. Funerals can be held in churches or funeral homes. Sometimes a viewing is held before the funeral. The viewing offers people a chance to see the deceased's body and confirm the reality of death.

A religious funeral includes prayers for the deceased and his or her loved

A funeral service takes place at the church at Beagle Bay Mission, in Western Australia.

ones, as well as religious music and readings. A religious leader, or someone who knew the deceased personally, may offer a eulogy in which he or she talks about the deceased's life. Nonreligious ceremonies also often include eulogies and a time for family and friends to say goodbye.

After the funeral, the body is usually buried in a church or city cemetery. A gathering also may occur after the funeral to give loved ones a chance to talk with others and share stories about the person who died. The gathering may simply mean a cup of tea and a biscuit at the family's home or refreshments at a local club, depending on the family's wishes.

Australia's current minimum wage for people who are at least 21 years old is 13.27 Australian dollars (U.S.$10.45). For those who are younger, 10 percent is subtracted for every year they are under the age of 21.

5 Making Money

AUSTRALIAN TEENAGERS LIVING IN CITIES COMMONLY GET THEIR FIRST JOBS OUTSIDE THEIR HOMES WHEN THEY ARE 14 OR 15. They may work part time in fast-food restaurants, movie theaters, or shopping malls, or they may have clerical positions.

In 2004, according to the Australian Bureau of Statistics, 36 percent of teenagers between the ages of 15 and 19 were working part time and studying full time. Whether a teen can have a part-time job while in school depends on whether the teen's parents approve of the idea, and on the economic situation of the family. Some families struggle to pay for school

Australia Industry Chart

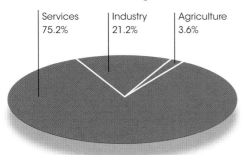

| Services 75.2% | Industry 21.2% | Agriculture 3.6% |

Source: United States Central Intelligence Agency. *The World Factbook—Australia.*

Teens who live on stations in the Outback are expected to help with daily chores.

supplies and transportation, and teens help support their families by working.

There are more than 64 Technical and Further Education institutions (TAFEs) and many other publicly funded organizations that provide training for students who leave school after year 10. These institutions are very important for young people because they prepare teens for jobs in a variety of areas such as education, health, transportation, and mechanical, electrical, and automotive engineering.

Work in the Outback

Teens who live in the Outback are expected to help with work at home.

Male teens who are hired to help on stations are called *jackeroos,* and females are called *jilleroos.* Workdays on the stations are long, and they

jackeroos
JACK-eh-roows

jilleroos
JILL-eh-roows

TAFEs

Technical and Further Education (TAFE) schools offer many courses in technical or vocational areas. They may include hospitality, tourism, construction, secretarial skills, and community work. TAFEs are funded and operated by the state and territory governments of Australia. (Regular universities are controlled by the federal government.) Many TAFE programs use the name "institute" rather than "college" to differentiate themselves from secondary-level colleges.

The first technical school in Australia was the Sydney Mechanics' School of Arts in 1883. After World War I (1914–1918), technical education was offered for free to veterans. During the Depression of the 1930s, classes were offered to occupy the unemployed and to perhaps create job opportunities. During World War II (1939–1945), workers, especially women, were trained to fill traditionally male roles for the war effort. The name TAFE was adopted in the 1970s. Today there are at least 64 TAFE schools throughout Australia.

The highest degree that can be earned from a TAFE institution is an advanced diploma, which is below a bachelor's degree. Often TAFE study can be used as partial credit toward bachelor degree-level university programs. Some TAFE schools also offer an Open Training and Education Network (OTEN), a form of distance education.

TAFE Certificates & Diplomas

An idea about how the TAFE system works can be seen in the following qualifications framework:

Qualification	Duration	Career Path
Certificate I	4–6 months	Competent operator
Certificate II	6–8 months	Advanced operator
Certificate III	About 12 months	Qualified tradesperson or technician
Certificate IV	12–18 months	Supervisor
Diploma	18–24 months	Paraprofessional
Advanced Diploma	24–36 months	Junior manager

Source: Australian Education Network.

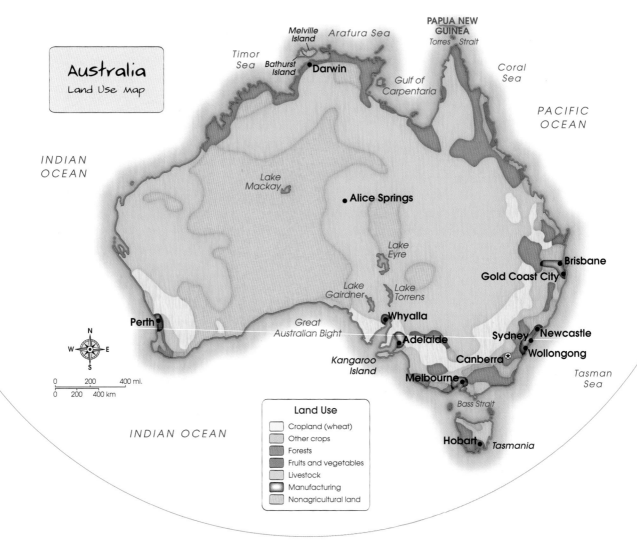

Australia
Land Use Map

PAPUA NEW GUINEA

Arafura Sea

Timor Sea

Melville Island

Bathurst Island

•Darwin

Torres Strait

Coral Sea

Gulf of Carpentaria

PACIFIC OCEAN

INDIAN OCEAN

Lake Mackay

•Alice Springs

Lake Eyre

•Brisbane

Gold Coast City•

Lake Gairdner

Lake Torrens

Perth•

Great Australian Bight

Whyalla

Sydney• •Newcastle

Adelaide•

Canberra ✪ •Wollongong

Kangaroo Island

Melbourne•

Tasman Sea

INDIAN OCEAN

Bass Strait

Land Use
☐ Cropland (wheat)
☐ Other crops
☐ Forests
☐ Fruits and vegetables
☐ Livestock
☐ Manufacturing
☐ Nonagricultural land

Hobart• Tasmania

N W E S

0   200   400 mi.
0   200   400 km

often include difficult, dirty work, such as feeding cattle and sheep. Chores often begin at sunrise and may last until sunset or later. These days, getting around on huge stations is more likely accomplished with four-wheel-drive and off-road vehicles rather than horses. Both cattle and sheep are raised on these stations, and one of the jobs a

teenager can train for is a sheep shearer. A skilled shearer can remove the wool from more than 150 sheep a day, but it takes a great deal of experience to get to that level.

Careers
Although many Outback teens go on to boarding school for their high school education, the number going on to

Recenty, about 33 percent of year 12 students chose to continue their studies at universities. About 22 percent chose TAFEs, about 4 percent chose other institutions, and about 28 percent chose to work full time. About 13 percent chose none of those options.

a university is not as great as for city teens. This is a problem that the government wants to address. More Australian teenagers are pursuing higher education now than teens did 20 years ago. Students tend to go to a university in their hometown. Nearly all stay in Australia for their undergraduate degrees, though more go overseas for graduate school to earn advanced degrees in hopes of getting better jobs.

Many Australian university students take a year off after finishing their education. They often use this time to travel to various parts of the world, including Southeast Asia, North America, and Great Britain and other areas of Europe. This year of travel is very important to young Australians and they look forward to it. Some stay and work in these countries if they can find jobs.

Manly Wharf in Sydney is a popular place for teens to gather and hang out, shop, or eat.

6 Hanging Out

AUSTRALIAN TEENS HAVE MANY WAYS TO SPEND TIME WHEN THEY aren't working or going to school. One activity they enjoy is going to the movies. The Harry Potter movies are as eagerly awaited as the books. And Johnny Depp and the Pirates of the Caribbean movies are sweeping the country as well.

Teens also enjoy reading. Along with the Harry Potter series, mysteries are popular books among teens, as are books about surfing. Teens also like books written by a variety of Australian authors. Isobelle Carmody writes exciting fantasy books that appeal to both teachers and students. Paul Jennings, Australia's

Some of the most popular books among Australian teens are fantasies, action/adventures, and mysteries.

most popular author, writes for children ages 5 through 15. His stories are funny and often feature strange twists at the end. One of Australia's most popular science fiction authors is Victor Kelleher, who also writes fantasy fiction for teenagers. John Marsden reigns as Australia's most popular author of books for teenagers. His series *The Tomorrow When the War Began* details the adventures of a group of teenagers forced to fight for their country when Australia is invaded by foreigners. It is the most popular series for young adults ever written in Australia.

Teens love magazines, too. Some of the most popular magazines are *Girlfriend*, *Dolly*, *TV Hits*, and *Surf*

Role Models

Popular sports stars and actors who teens look up to include:

Ian Thorpe

Nicknamed Thorpedo, Ian Thorpe is considered one of the world's best freestyle swimmers of all time. In 1997, he became the youngest member of Australia's national swim team at age 14. During his career he captured five Olympic gold medals and 11 world championships, breaking 22 world records in the process. He retired in November 2006. Outside of the pool, he runs a foundation that sponsors health and education programs for children throughout the world.

Layne Beachley

Considered the best female surfer in history, Layne Beachley started surfing professionally at age 16. She has 29 wins on the world championship tour, and has been named the world champion for six consecutive years. She sponsors Aim for the Stars, a foundation that supports girls and women in reaching academic, athletic, or professional goals.

John Eales

Many rugby fans call John Eales the most successful Australian captain of all time. He helped Australia earn two World Cups in 1991 and 1999. Each year, the best Australian Rugby Union player is awarded a medal in his name.

Hugh Jackman

Teens love Hugh Jackman for his role as Wolverine in the *X-Men* films. The native Australian has also starred in numerous stage productions in Australia, London, and New York. In 2004, he won a Tony award for his Broadway performance as another famous Australian, singer Peter Allen, in the musical *The Boy from Oz*.

Actress Nicole Kidman is known for her nearly 50 film roles. In 2003, she won the Academy Award for best actress. Kidman serves as UNICEF Australia's Goodwill Ambassador. In this role, she helps raise money and awareness for disadvantaged children in Australia.

Life. The Helix is one of the favorite magazines for younger teens who are interested in science.

While teens enjoy watching and reading about movie stars and rock musicians, they most often look closer to home when searching for role models. Teens often point to their parents and other adults in their lives as having the most influence on them.

Dating

Many teens do not really date until their last year of high school, if even then. Teens love to go out in groups, and they spend a great deal of time on the phone organizing activities. Messages about plans for an evening or for the weekend are passed from one person in the group to the next.

For teens who are at least 18 years old, the legal drinking age in Australia, a get-together may involve going to a club or party where alcohol is served. If that is the case, teens choose a designated driver before they leave for the event. The designated driver will not drink that night and makes sure everyone gets home safely. Australia has random breath testing, and those caught

There are 18.2 million cell phones in use throughout Australia.

drinking and driving receive severe penalties, including seeing their names published in the newspaper.

Vacations

Teens enjoy holidays, or vacations, and they find no shortage of ways to occupy themselves. School holidays are often times for families to do things together. Many families head for a summer cottage at the beach or go camping at one of the many campgrounds that dot the Australian coastline.

In the cities, teens can visit zoos

A mother and son camp near Shoalhaven River, in New South Wales.

during their free time. In Sydney, Featherdale Wildlife Park lets visitors hand-feed a kangaroo. Featherdale also gives visitors a chance to have their picture taken with a koala.

Another popular zoo in Australia is Sydney's Taronga Zoo. Along with African and Asian animals such as elephants, lions, and monkeys, Tarongo houses a variety of Australian animals, including the kookaburra—a bird with a "laughing" call—and platypus.

A child at Featherdale Wildlife Park feeds a kangaroo.

HANGING OUT

A popular place for Australians to visit is the Royal Botanical Garden in Melbourne.

In Melbourne, Victoria, the Royal Botanical Garden draws thousands of visitors. A peaceful place along the Yarra River, the garden includes 88 acres (35.2 hectares) of native and exotic plants, including ferns and a cactus garden. A popular place for families, the garden offers picnic areas and open spaces for children to play. During the summer, the garden hosts outdoor theater performances and shows movies by moonlight.

Kakadu National Park, in the Northern Territory, is a popular spot for families to camp. Kakadu includes more than 5,100 square miles (13,260 sq km) of breathtaking cliffs, swamps and wildlife. Those who want a less rustic vacation experience can rent one of many cottages along the pristine beach.

A Wildlife All Its Own

Australian plants and animals have developed in isolation from plants and animals on other continents. As a result, they have evolved to fit the unique climate and landscape of their homeland. That is why many types of plants and animals are found only in Australia.

The kangaroo is a common marsupial that is unique to Australia. The kangaroo is one of Australia's national symbols, and the government has passed laws to protect them. However, the government sometimes allows hunters to apply for licenses to hunt kangaroos in order to protect crops or to obtain meat and leather. Along with being a nuisance for farmers, kangaroos can prove dangerous to people driving in the country after the sun goes down. Kangaroos are most active at night, when they are drawn to the road because it holds the heat from the day. People who often travel country roads at night may have special bull bars attached to the fronts of their cars. The bull bar protects a vehicle from serious damage should it hit a kangaroo.

Wallabies and koalas are other marsupials found only in Australia. Wallabies look like their close relatives, the kangaroo. Koalas may look like cuddly teddy bears, but they have sharp, curved claws. Koalas spend most of their days in the forks of eucalyptus trees, their main source of food and water.

More noticeable for its unusual call than its coloring, the kookaburra is a bird unique to Australia.

Kookaburras "laugh like a human—if you have a bizarre laugh!" said 14-year-old Brooke Hill,

Australia also has many dangerous animals that people don't want to encounter. The country is home to more venomous snakes than any other nation in the world. More than 30 kinds of poisonous sea snakes are found there. On land, another 30 venomous snakes slither around. Among them is the taipan, the deadliest snake on Earth. Taipans are dark brown to black on top, but underneath they are a creamy yellow with orange spots. Most are less than 7 feet (2 meters) long, but they can grow to lengths of more than 10 feet (3 m), making taipans one of the largest and most feared poisonous snakes on the continent. However, most snakes prefer to sneak away rather than attack. As a result, people rarely see these deadly snakes.

Along the coast of northern Australia, swimmers must watch out for the box jellyfish. They are usually found during the wet season, which runs from October until April. Box jellyfish are difficult to see because they are transparent. However, if a swimmer encounters one, he or she will know it right away. A single sting from a box jellyfish is so painful that a person may go into shock and drown before the full effect of the venom sets in. As a result, beaches are closed when box jellyfish are found in the waters.

The platypus is found in freshwater areas of eastern Australia and is protected throughout the country.

Although many people refer to koalas as bears, they are marsupials.

Queensland is the most popular state for Australians on holiday. It is known for its beautiful, sandy beaches, lush rain forests, and tropical islands.

Sports

Australia is an athletic nation. Nearly 13 million Australians ages 15 and older participate in some physical activity, such as playing on a sports team or exercising for fun. About 11 million people exercise at least once a week. More than 4 million people exercise at least five times per week.

The opportunities for recreational sports are limitless. The country's mountains offer opportunities for hiking in the summer and skiing in the winter. The nation's beaches attract swimmers, surfers, sailors, and scuba divers.

But Australia's national sport is Australian rules football. This game combines aspects of American football, soccer, and rugby. It is played with

An Australian rules footballer lines up the goals on the field.

Australian Rules Football

Similar to football in the United States, Australian rules football is a rough, hard-hitting sport that tests the strength and agility of the players. Australian rules football (also known as "Aussie rules" or "footy") is played on an oval-shaped field with a standard range of 148½ yards (135 m) wide and 181½ yards (165 m) long. At each end of the field there are two goal posts and a behind post next to each goal post. The ball is made of leather and is shaped like a U.S. football, but the ends are rounded instead of pointed. Each footy team can have 15 players on the field at one time. The game begins much like a jump ball in a basketball game. In footy, though, the umpire bounces the ball off the ground before the players can tip it to a teammate.

Handling the ball in footy is tricky. If players run with the ball, they have to bounce the ball or touch it to the ground every 16½ yards (15 m). Although players can hold the ball (without moving forward) for any amount of time, players have to release the ball if tackled or held by an opposing player. Players cannot pass the ball; instead, they perform a handball, which is holding the ball in one hand and using the other hand to hit it with a closed fist. The players have four quarters, each 20 minutes long, in which to score points for their team. There are two ways to score points in footy. First, if the ball is kicked through the goal posts, the team gets six points. All other scoring is worth a behind, or one point. There are many ways to score a behind, such as carrying the ball through the goal posts, kicking the ball between a goal post and a behind, or hitting the goal post with the ball. The team with the most points when time runs out is the winner.

an oval ball on an oval field. Played during the winter, football attracts more spectators than any other sporting event in the country. It is particularly popular in Melbourne. About one of every 16 people living in Melbourne attends a football game on an average Saturday. Thousands more gather around their televisions to watch this rough sport, which is unique to their nation.

Rugby ranks as another popular winter sport. Children as young as 5 can belong to a rugby team. Younger kids play a noncontact version of the game. Teens play the sport through school clubs. The object of a rugby match is for a team to move the ball down the field by passing, kicking, or grounding it. The team that scores the most points by getting the ball into the opposing team's end zone wins.

Since the 19th century, cricket has been a popular summer sport. Most teenagers enjoy playing or watching it. The game is played with a wide, flat bat and a hard red ball that is a little bigger than a baseball. Children who use plastic equipment play a form of cricket called "Kanga Cricket."

Australian rugby fans celebrated a World Cup victory in 1999 and settled for second place in 2003.

Looking Ahead

LIKE THE REST OF THE POPULATION, AUSTRALIAN TEENS ARE A MIX OF PEOPLE—FROM THE NATIVE ABORIGINES TO THE DESCENDANTS OF THE BRITISH SETTLERS AND THE MILLIONS OF IMMIGRANTS WHO HAVE FLOCKED TO THE NATION IN RECENT DECADES. Each group has brought its values, beliefs, and traditions with it, creating a way of life unique to Australia.

Many Australian teens live social lifestyles. They love spending time with family and friends. That may involve hanging around the backyard barbie, heading to the beach to swim and surf, or driving to the movie theater to catch the latest flick. In the Outback, teens find their choices more limited, but they still enjoy spending time with their families after a long day of hard work.

More than ever, the future for all teens in Australia is one that is not only bright, but also achievable. Australians have risen to the challenges that their country has faced. They have devised ways to make sure everyone has opportunities to obtain such important things as education and health care, regardless of where they live.

Official name: Commonwealth of Australia

Capital: Canberra

People

Population: 20,264,082

Population by age group:
0-14 years: 19.6%
15-64 years: 67.3%
65 years and over: 13.1%

Life expectancy at birth: 80.5 years

Official language: English

Other languages: Chinese, Italian, many indigenous languages

Religions:
Roman Catholic: 26.4%
Anglican: 20.5%
Other Christian: 20.5%
Buddhist: 1.9%
Muslim: 1.5%
Other: 1.2%
Unspecified: 12.7%
None: 15.3%

Legal ages:
Alcohol consumption: 18
Driver's license: learner's permit at 16½, full license at 18
Employment: no minimum
Marriage: 16
Military service: voluntary beginning at age 16
Voting: 18

Government

Type of government: Democratic, federal-state system recognizing British monarch as sovereign

Chief of state: Queen

Head of government: Prime minister, deputy prime minister; following legislative elections, the leader of the majority party or leader of a majority coalition becomes prime minister.

Lawmaking body: Federal Parliament consisting of the Senate and the House of Representatives, elected by popular vote

Administrative divisions: Six states and two territories

Independence: January 1, 1901

National symbols: Golden wattle, the opal, and the kangaroo and emu (the latter two found on the country's coat of arms)

Geography

Total area: 3,074,740 square miles (7,994,324 square kilometers)

Climate: Generally arid to semiarid; temperate in south and east; tropical in north

Highest point: Mount Kosciuszko, 7,355.7 feet (2,243 meters)

Lowest point: Lake Eyre, 49½ feet (15 meters)

Major landforms: Gibson Desert, Great Victoria Desert, Simpson Desert, Tanami Desert, Nullarbor Plain, Kimberley Plateau, Barkly Tableland, Great Artesian Basin,

Darling Range, Great Dividing Range, Gregory Range, Hamersley Range, King Leopold Ranges, MacDonnell Ranges, Robinson Ranges, Uluru

Major river: Murray

Economy

Currency: Australian dollar

Major natural resources: Bauxite, coal, iron ore, copper, tin, gold, silver, uranium, nickel, tungsten, mineral sands, lead, zinc, diamonds, natural gas, petroleum

Major agricultural products: Wheat, barley, sugarcane, fruits, cattle, sheep, poultry

Major exports: Coal, gold, meat, alumina, iron ore, wheat, machinery, transportion equipment

Major imports: Machinery and transportation equipment, computers and office machines, telecommunication equipment and parts, crude oil, petroleum products

Historical Timeline

 Women gain voting privileges in New Zealand, the first country to take such a step

 The Maya rise to prominence in Central America

Captain James Cook sails to the east coast of Australia and claims it for England

Gold is discovered in several locations leading to gold rushes; the population tops 1 million; Aborigines are treated badly and their numbers decline sharply

40,000 B.C.	250 A.D.	1519–1522	1770	1788	1793	1850s	1893

First Aborigines arrive in Australia from southeast Asia

The first free settlers begin arriving

Ferdinand Magellan attempts voyage around the world; he dies but crew completes the trip

About 800 convicts are sent from Great Britain to Australia, which will be used as a penal colony; the Aboriginal population is several hundred thousand

Historical World Event

The capital city of
Canberra is founded

The Australia Act
makes Australian law
independent of the
British Parliament
and legal system

 The U.S. stock market
crashes, and severe
worldwide economic
depression sets in

The first personal
computer in the
world is introduced

1901   1913   1914–1918   1929   1939–1945   1956   1981   1986

The country is unified and
the Commonwealth of
Australia is created on
January 1

Melbourne hosts the
Olympic Games

Australian
troops fight in
World War II

Australian
troops fight in
World War I

Historical Timeline

The UN releases a report that declares Norway, Iceland, Australia, Ireland, and Sweden as the best five countries in which to live

Sydney hosts the Olympic Games

 The Soviet Union collapses

Riots break out between police and Aboriginal residents in suburban Sydney after an Aboriginal teen is killed; racially motivated violence, involving thousands of youth, hits Sydney the following year

| 1989 | 1991 | 1993 | 2000 | 2001 | 2002 | 2004 | 2006 |

Farmers are devastated by the worst drought in 100 years; water restrictions are ordered in many cities

The Native Title Act establishes a process for the granting of Aboriginal land rights

 The Berlin Wall falls

 Terrorist attacks on the two World Trade Center Towers in New York City and on the Pentagon in Washington, D.C., leave thousands dead

Glossary

Aborigines | members of the indigenous people of Australia

apprentice | someone who learns a trade by working with a person already skilled in the job

cyclones | storms or systems of winds that rotate around a center of low atmospheric pressure and often bring heavy rainfall

electives | courses that students can choose to take but are not required

indigenous | native to a place

kiosks | small structures with one or more open sides

marsupial | group of mammals in which the females feed and carry their young in pouches

monsoons | weather seasons characterized by very heavy rainfall

nomadic | relating to roaming around aimlessly from place to place

Outback | the rural and arid interior region of Australia

seminomadic | relating to a migrant lifestyle, in which people move with the seasons and work

tuition | fee paid to attend a school

Additional Resources

IN THE LIBRARY

Banting, Erinn. *Australia: The Culture*.
New York: Crabtree, 2003.

Banting, Erinn. *Australia: The People*.
New York: Crabtree, 2003.

Bartlett, Anne. *The Aboriginal Peoples
of Australia*. Minneapolis, Minn.:
Learner Publications, 2002.

Darlington, Robert. *Australia*. Austin,
Texas: Raintree Steck-Vaughn, 2001.

Einfeld, Jann. *Life in the Australian Outback*.
San Diego: Lucent Books, 2003.

Jordan-Bychkov, Terry G. *Australia*.
Philadelphia, Pa.: Chelsea House
Publishers, 2003.

Kerns, Ann. *Australia in Pictures*.
Minneapolis, Minn.: Learner
Publications, 2004.

ON THE WEB

For more information on this topic, use
FactHound.
1. Go to www.facthound.com
2. Type in this book ID: 0756524415
3. Click on the *Fetch It* button.

Look for more Global Connections books.

Teens in Brazil
Teens in China
Teens in France
Teens in India
Teens in Israel
Teens in Japan
Teens in Kenya

Teens in Mexico
Teens in Russia
Teens in Saudi Arabia
Teens in Spain
Teens in Venezuela
Teens in Vietnam

Source Notes

Page 13, column 2, line 13: Rhiannon Hughes. E-mail interview. 1 July 2006.

Page 15, column 2, line 11: Michelle Glossop. E-mail interview. 6 July 2006.

Page 16, column 2, line 1: Rhiannon Hughes.

Page 24, column 1, line 8: Michelle Glossop.

Page 25, column 1, line 3: Rhiannon Hughes.

Page 36, column 1, line 7: Ibid.

Page 46, column 1, line 3: Jeffrey Pike, ed. *Australia*. Maspeth, N.Y.: Langenscheidt Publishers, Inc., 2004, p. 79.

Page 48, column 1, line 16: Michelle Glossop.

Page 48, column 1, line 29: Rhiannon Hughes.

Page 53, column 1, line 4: Ibid.

Page 76, Column 2, line 12: Brooke Hill. E-mail interview. 1 July 2006.

Pages 84–85, At a Glance: United States. Central Intelligence Agency. *The World Factbook—Australia*. 30 Nov. 2006. 6 Dec. 2006. https://www.cia.gov/cia/publications/factbook/geos/as.html

Select Bibliography

Australian Education Network. 13 Dec. 2006. Australian-universities.com/colleges

Australian Institute of Marine Science. 7 Dec. 2006. www.aims.gov.au/index.html

Bernstein, Ken. *Australia*. London, England: Berlitz Publishing, 2003.

Commonwealth of Australia. Australian Bureau of Statistics. 18 Oct. 2006. 7 Dec. 2006. www.abs.gov.au/

Commonwealth of Australia. Australian Electoral Commission. 18 Oct. 2006. 7 Dec. 2006. www.aec.gov.au/

Commonwealth of Australia. Australian Embassy. 7 Dec. 2006. www.austemb.org/

Commonwealth of Australia. Australian Government. *Australian Culture and the Arts*. 7 Dec. 2006. www.dfat.gov.au/facts/culture_arts.html

Commonwealth of Australia. High Court of Australia. 7 Dec. 2006. www.hcourt.gov.au/

Commonwealth of Australia. Office of the Prime Minister. John Howard. 7 Dec. 2006. www.pm.gov.au/index.cfm Australian Government Culture and Recreation Portal. *Australian Weather and the Seasons*. www.cultureandrecreation.gov.au/articles/weather/

Great Barrier Reef Australia. 7 Dec. 2006. www.barrierreefaustralia.com/

Macintyre, Stuart. *A Concise History of Australia*. New York: Cambridge University Press, 2004.

Penney, Barry. *Australia*. Portland, Ore.: Graphic Arts Center Publishing Co., 2003.

Pike, Jeffrey, ed. *Australia*. Maspeth, N.Y.: Langenscheidt Publishers Inc., 2004.

"School Information." Alice Springs School of the Air. 18 Oct. 2006. 7 Dec. 2006. www.assoa.nt.edu.au/_SCHOOL%20INFORMATION/schoolinfo.html

"The Services Provided." Royal Flying Doctor Service. 7 Dec. 2006. www.flyingdoctor.net/services.htm

Sharp, Ilsa. *Culture Shock!: Australia*. Singapore: Times Books International, 1992.

Smith, Roff Martin. *Australia: Journey Through a Timeless Land*. Washington, D.C.: National Geographic, 1999.

Smith, Roff Martin. *Cold Beer and Crocodiles: A Bicycle Journey into Australia*. Washington, D.C.: Adventure Press, National Geographic, 2000.

Terrill, Ross. *The Australians*. New York: Simon and Schuster, 1987.

United States Central Intelligence Agency. *The World Factbook—Australia*. 12 Dec. 2006. 14. Dec. 2006. www.cia.gov/cia/publications/factbook/geos/as.html

Index

About the Author
Brenda Haugen

Brenda Haugen started in the newspaper business and had a career as an award-winning journalist before finding her niche as an author. Since then, she has written and edited many books, most of them for children. A graduate of the University of North Dakota in Grand Forks, Brenda lives in North Dakota with her family.

About the Content Adviser
Frances F. Cushing

Frances F. Cushing currently works as a research associate for the Edward A. Clark Center for Australian and New Zealand Studies at the University of Texas at Austin. She was a reference librarian in the Federal Parliamentary Library in Canberra for 20 years, returning to the United States in 1993. While living in Australia, Cushing and her husband raised two boys. As our adviser on *Teens in Australia*, she was able to personally contact Australian acquaintances to confirm details about current teen life in Australia.